AF413594

Praise for

17 STRANDS

"This book reminds us that participation alone does not change systems. What changes outcomes is sustained, grounded action and willingness to take responsibility when we still have another chance to make better decisions."

—Corinna Hawkes

Director, Agrifood Systems and Food Safety Division for the Food and Agriculture Organization of the United Nations

"In 17 Strands: Weaving Local Courage to Global Change, Joseph Bangura delivers a compelling and timely reflection on a new generation of leaders boldly navigating the intersection of local realities and global influence. With clarity, conviction, and purpose, he highlights the transformative power of youth agency in shaping both national narratives and the broader international discourse. This work stands as both an inspiration and a call to action for emerging leaders determined to drive meaningful change."

—His Excellency Ambassador Sidique Abou-Bakarr Wai

Former Ambassador of Sierra Leone to the United States (2019-2025)

What can you weave when you have nothing but yourself?

17 STRANDS

Weaving Local Courage Into Global Change

J&N Press

For people who feel the SDGs but don't speak them fluently.
For young leaders who want permission to act imperfectly.
For changemakers who are doing the work quietly and wondering
if anyone else is out there.

ACKNOWLEDGEMENT

I would like to express my gratitude to Corinna Hawkes — Director of Agrifood System and Food Safety Division at the Food and Agriculture Organization of the United Nations — for her insightful words, which not only serve as a constant reminder to our commitment to a sustainable world, but also anchors and embodies the essence of 17 STRANDS. Thank you to His Excellency, Ambassador Sidique Aboubakarr Wai, the former Ambassador of Sierra Leone to the United States, who has always been a role model for young people nationally and globally. To the changemakers who submitted their stories of impact to be featured, I want to sincerely thank you for sharing your story. Your dedication, creativity, and courage inspire not only me, but all those who will read this book. Together our voices help shape a book that inspires, guides, and documents change, as well as reminding the world that hope is local. Thank you to Matthew Modine for providing the metaphor that inspired this book. And finally, thank you to my editor Noah Dennie, who challenged my thinking, helped me expand my vision, and ensured this book would truly resonate with the next generation of leaders.

CONTENTS

I. Preface

II. Acknowledgement

III. Introduction

Chapter 1: Beyond Participation: Why Youth Must Weave

Chapter 2: The Architecture of Connection: Mapping Your Web

Chapter 3: Moored: Weaving Through Fractured Threads

Epigraph: Corinna Hawkes

Chapter 4: The Weaver's Web: Stories of Local Courage

    i.   Mahlet Zeleke Redi

    ii.   Amboseli's Elites

    iii.   Rosaline Adewuyi

    iv.   Rita AwestiGodwin Kevin

    v.   Suzzane

    vi.   Arthurlina Johnson

    vii.   EasySTEM

Chapter 5: The Pivot: "We Have Another Shot at Making the Right Decision"

Chapter 6: The Language we Carry

EDITORIAL PREFACE

17 Strands is a testament to the dynamic interconnection of each individual. Its core message is this: *your actions count; you have an impact, whether you see it or not.* It is an attempt to humanize the policies and celebrate the efforts present in international spaces of cooperation, while also offering a glimpse into some of the challenges posed by those spaces for young leaders and advocates. The '17' comes from the seventeen Sustainable Development Goals set by the United Nations, an international council consisting of delegates from 193 countries. The 'Strands' evolved from a metaphor representing the systemic organization of ameliorative efforts and impact.

Joseph Bangura is a young man from Sierra Leone who got involved in his community to make circumstances better for other people. Eventually, he came to the United States where his work connected him to the United Nations. In his experience as a young changemaker, navigating this new high-level forum, while also remaining dedicated to his cause, he has gained a wealth of experience which he wants to impart to others. He shares insights from this experience about misrepresentation, the sway of political decorum, and the barriers in place that other young changemakers may encounter on their respective journeys.

This book is also meant to educate and raise awareness about the 17 Sustainable Development Goals (SDGs) that have been established. Though there are several distinct goals, one of the central themes of the book is that each goal is interconnected with at least one other goal; when an effort is made in the domain of one goal, it resonates and has an impact in the domain of another. A significant portion of the book is dedicated to the stories of other young changemakers who have shared their narrative and their efforts in progressing towards the 17 SDGs, followed by a brief analysis of how their efforts have had scaled impact towards the goals. In upraising these narratives, this book aims to celebrate their actions and demonstrate to other youth that change begins locally, as community members who take action, which then compound over time through cooperation and perseverance.

At the end of the book, there are a few pages dedicated to encourage those who want to have an impact on the goals. It makes use of concepts discussed in the book and engages readers to brainstorm or develop and plan for how they can begin taking action to make circumstances better in their communities.

INTRODUCTION

In a fast-paced world where everyone wants to be handed the microphone, where the microphone itself feels like currency, many actions have become a means to an end and collaboration has always suffered. Not because young people or leaders lack passion, but because the ecosystem often rewards visibility over impact. It pushes young leaders into competition when we should be consciously choosing collaboration. Yet, while the world evolves, millions are still being left behind.

When we forget to collaborate, we neglect those we have taken the stage to represent. Some die of starvation and war. Others lack access to quality education, clean water, medicine, or equal rights. And in this overwhelming noise, you may find yourself asking: *Is there any love and compassion left? Will there be leaders who truly care? Is there still hope? Are there real-life heroes?*

Growing up in Sierra Leone, I was involved in changemaking and policy work, from educating youth, engaging with broadcasting stations, speaking on behalf of government health, and founding an organization to boost sustainable food equity. I continued this work throughout my education, which led me to the United States, and offered me the opportunity to further engage with the United Nations. I was involved with the Youth Association of Sierra Leone and the United Nations Major Group for Children and Youth, both of which are in consultation with the United Nations Economic and Social Council. From this position, I was invited to several speaking events and UN meetings concerning policy, one of which was at the Peace Boat Blue Innovation Reception.

During one of the most unexpected yet meaningful encounters of my journey — I interviewed Award winning actor and Ocean Advocate Matthew Modine, whom some of you might know from the Netflix series *Stranger Things*. Our conversation was not about Hollywood, it was about survival, collaboration, and the moral duty of those with a platform. I asked *him, how do we stay steadfast and hold the fort? What should we do when global leaders' visions do not align with building a sustainable world? What do we do when those in power, those with the resources, seem to be disconnected from the future we are fighting for, making us feel like we are in pursuit of a 'pie in the sky' dream?* He shared a metaphor that has never left me and I am convinced is part of the moral lessons that shape this book.

The metaphor encompasses a spider web. Paraphrasing Mr. Modine, at first glance, the web looks fragile — easy to tear apart — but in reality, a spider web is incredibly strong because every thread works together to hold the structure. The tension of one strand is distributed throughout the whole web. And even when part of the web is damaged, the spider does not abandon it. It repairs it. It reinforces it. It keeps building.

Our world is like that web. Leadership may fail. Systems may weaken. Policies may lag behind reality, but as long as ordinary people — young people, communities, teachers, advocates — continue to hold their thread, the world does not collapse. We keep reinforcing hope. We keep strengthening what matters. We keep building forward. We collaborate, support one another, and recognize that our struggles and victories are intertwined. The web holds, and humanity stands a chance.

After reflecting on Matthew Modine's words, I had an epiphany and insight: like the spider web, the seventeen Sustainable Development Goals (SDGs) of the United Nations, are not separated, but rather they are interdependent, interconnected, and only powerful when they work together. We cannot talk about goal one which is "No Poverty" without talking about goal four

(Quality Education) because poverty is connected to education the same way health is connected to climate, and peace connected to partnership. None of these goals exist in isolation; they are threads woven into survival and the future of our world. Pull one thread, whether it be poverty, climate, health, peace, or education, and everything else shifts. Strengthen one thread, and the entire structure grows stronger. This is the world's promise to itself: a commitment to make sure no child goes hungry, no dream dies because of poverty, and no community is left behind.

That metaphor reminded me of the importance of the Sustainable Development Goals, and that greatness in leadership is not always loud, glamorous, positioned at the top, or about one individual. It is about all of us and sometimes, it looks like people are quietly, and persistently strengthening their corner of the world so the whole web can stay intact, instead of looking for the microphone.

So, while some of you might believe heroes only exist in movies — on giant screens, wearing capes, saving cities, what if I reminded you there is still hope, that there's a lot of love and compassion left to give? What if I reminded you there are still future thoughtful leaders in our world? Some you've heard of in whispers, or seen scrolling on social media; others you've passed by without realizing their strength. You have even met a few, but never truly recognized for who they are – and they may not either.

These heroes are out there, spread across the globe, creating positive change in their communities. The rest are waiting to be inspired and activated. This book is about them and their individual adventures for a better tomorrow — the young, the brave, the ordinary who dared to dream, fight, and stood the test of time. In every corner of the world, their stories are unfolding. And now… you get to meet them.

17 STRANDS is not a manual for solving the world's problems. It's an orientation and a re-orientation toward a structural gap between global commitment and local consequences. Think of it like navigating an unfamiliar terrain: if your map tells you there is a bridge, but your eyes see a canyon, you do not argue with the ground. You stop. You reassess. You re-orient.

This book lives in that moment. It aims to activate a generation of proactive do-ers through relatable narratives, visual storytelling, and global inclusion. It inspires action while documenting impact. What sets it apart is its reach across continents, its use of story as strategy, and its focus on activating leadership from the ground up.

Lastly, unlike traditional awareness campaigns, it blends storytelling, education, and activism in a format designed for youth — by youth. It translates global goals into local human stories. It celebrates youth's potential to spark change. It's a mirror for young people to see their power through others while creating value-based movement around purpose, impact, legacy, and hope. It's a call to action.

The world needs fewer performers and more builders. If you were to ask me, "How did you do it?" — this book has the answer. Let your impact speak louder than your voice. And know you can begin right where you are.

<u>**CHAPTER 1**</u>

Beyond Participation: Why Youth Must Weave

Over the couple of years I have walked into global rooms where change was discussed, I have seen how microphones passed hands like trophies, and where speaking became the prize. But I realized something important: impact matters more than appearances. Some people chase platforms. Others build them with consistency, with compassion, and with quiet acts that ripple beyond what a mic can reach.

I have also met young people through social interactions or on platforms like Instagram, and at speaking engagements where I was invited to — such as the International Youth Conference, the United Nations ECOSOC Partnership Forum, ECOSOC Youth Forum and High-Level Political Forum — asking me *"What are the sustainable development goals? How do you do it? Where do I start?"* I have walked this path before, rising from a small classroom in Sierra Leone as a volunteer teacher to UN global stages as a youth ambassador and speaker, advocating for change with no roadmap, while grappling to fully understand what the SDGs are all about. This makes me wonder: *does SDG education exist in schools? Are they adult-centered, jargon-heavy, or too policy-driven? Have the current solutions largely failed to empower young people with practical skills for grassroots change?* If so, this leaves a critical gap between awareness and impactful action, fostering disempowerment.

But have you ever had that gut-wrenching feeling that something is fundamentally wrong and you should stand up against it? It could be in your community, school, neighborhood, and even in social gatherings. Oprah Winfrey calls it *the whispers of life* or *life whispers*. She said in her book, The Path Made Clear, "It's a quiet nudge from deep within saying, *Hmm, something feels off*. A small voice that tells you, *This is no longer your place of belonging…*" (Winfrey 44).

That is something I have felt. I felt it while walking down the street and saw a grown man treat a public corner like a private latrine. I felt it the first day I got into college in 2018, and a lecturer said, *"I suffered when I got into college, it is your turn"*, and when some of my friends sat in silent tears, complaining about lecturers who demanded money or their bodies for a passing grade. I felt it in the classroom in high school where Agricultural Science was nothing more than a long list of miscellaneous topics memorized for exams with no practical learning, no real-world connection, nothing that could truly feed a nation. I felt it when I walked outside my grandmother's house a few years ago and the air had a thick grey, choking smell of her neighbor's burning waste and plastic refuse — a weekly ritual due to the inexistence of a sufficient waste management system.

In each of these moments, I was not seeing SDGs, United Nations projects, or global agendas. I saw a problem, broken human realities — a human project. This human project is the catalyst of what propelled my interests. It's the source of origin and drive for the SDGs. What I was seeing was the thread that holds society together snapping under pressure. The man on the street was a break in sanitation. The lecturer was a break in justice and a strong institution. The burning waste was a break in our climate. And most people who look at these broken threads either feel helpless, or shrug and say, "That's just the way it is."

But it is not the way it has to be.

Oprah went on to say "Heeding these signs can open doors to your personal evolution, pushing you towards your life's purpose. Ignoring them — sleepwalking through life — is an invitation to chaos" (Winfrey 45). So, while I did not begin with SDGs, I leaned into that gut-wrenching feeling, that life whisper — began with human beings. The SDGs are just names the United Nations uses to make the problems measurable, but for you and me, they are the gut-wrenching feelings, the life whispers. They are the names for heartbreaks.

The United Nations calls it SDG 2 (Zero Hunger) but for you and me, it is the gut-wrenching feeling of watching a child in a war zone cry because their stomach is empty. SDG 5 (Gender Equality) is the heartbreak of female students experiencing lecturers demanding their bodies in exchange for passing grades. SDG 16 (Peace and Justice) is the anger and frustration you feel when innocent lives are extinguished in Gaza, Afghanistan, and Ukraine, realizing that peace is not just a goal on a poster, but a matter of survival. These goals are not abstract, they are real human suffering, and the urgency to act is palpable. We see the hunger in a child's eyes, the grief of lives lost to war, the fear and violation of those forced to trade their dignity for success and we cannot turn away. We feel it, we mourn it, and we fight for change.

If you noticed, I used the word "weave" and not "lead" in the chapter's title. While we do deserve a platform and a seat at the table, leadership in our current global system is often vertical, rigid — and if we are being honest — lonely. But weaving? Weaving is about the horizontal power of the strands. A single thread is easily snapped, but seventeen strands, woven with intention, can hold the weight of a planet.

Being invited to the room, being given the microphone for five minutes, and deciding how that microphone, that room, and the people inside it connect back to the dream of the village — connect to our common goals — has taught me something uncomfortable: that not every room filled with passionate leaders is filled with unity. And this is not only a problem among leaders at the top, but also among us too.

Many youth leaders I know, myself included, have felt it. I am not writing this from a place of perfection. I have made mistakes. I have chased platforms before I understood impact. I have competed when I should have collaborated. I have misunderstood, hesitated, doubted, and sometimes wanted to be at the "center of the web" myself. But growth is not about pretending to be flawless, it is about learning to step back, to listen, and to choose better the next time.

As I recall one of my speaking engagements at the United Nations High-Level Political Forum, where I spoke about having "another shot at making the right decision," it became clear to me that our role was not to stand at the center of the conversation, but to weave our reality and the realities of those we represent into it. The web is not designed for someone to stand at the center.

Real change is not built by a single name, face, or leader. It is built by many hands, hearts, and many threads working together. Yet too often, these spaces quietly become arenas of competition. Opportunities are limited, fellowships are few, speaking slots are prized, and suddenly the pursuit of impact begins to feel like a race. We congratulate each other publicly, but many of us are silently comparing who is getting recognized, invited into the important rooms, and who is seen as the face of change.

And this is not because young people are selfish. It is because many of us come from places where visibility feels like survival. Recognition feels like validation that our struggles, sacrifices, and work were worth it. In a world that constantly underestimates youth, we begin to believe we must constantly prove ourselves. But that logic assumes leadership is a pyramid. In a pyramid, the only way to get closer to the goal is to climb over someone else. This work however, was never meant to be built that way.

In a web, the goal sits at the heart, and our responsibility is not to ascend — but to reinforce, ensuring the strands are strong enough to hold us all. When we weave, we are reminded of the quiet, patient, act of connecting our individual local heartbreaks to a shared global pulse. When we remember that, leadership stops being a competition for the center and transforms into a collective act of care.

<h1 style="text-align:center"><u>CHAPTER 2</u></h1>

The Architecture of Connection: Mapping Your Web

The danger of global development is the blind node, a point of departure from local realities in policy rooms. At this blind node, there is a possibility for some policy makers to engage in discussions that do not properly map on to local realities or accurately represent the community's lived experience. Because efforts in high-level rooms are being made, we assume that the local reality and the policy reality being discussed are the same, but how many changemakers have checked the nuance between those two realities? Have we ensured that what is occurring locally is what is being represented globally? This is the notion of the 'data-reality gap'.

I believe as active youth leaders we all have found ourselves in a position where we are frustrated by the data-reality

gap, like the total absence of practical agriculture in schools —
despite official curriculum goals or official data saying agriculture
is being practiced. Though this is what is being represented, the
reality is that youth unemployment in this sector is still rising and
the import of food, like rice, is skyrocketing.

It makes you wonder if global strategy is built from top to
bottom. As youth leaders in global rooms, one of the many roles
we are often asked to play is that of the translator of local realities.
This is a role of observance and awareness of the underrepresented
communities where efforts are being made, which is a bottom to
top directed role. In achieving this, youth leaders become ground
truth validators, people who verify the nuance between the two
realities.

We are the people who have to live in the gap between
what the report says and what the reality looks like. In global
spaces, the language is polished, but behind every badge or event
pass on our chests, there are marginalized countries, cities, and
communities we each represent. It could be a village in Kenya
grappling with gender inequality. It could be a city like Gaza living
with a war crisis. It could be a school with no infrastructure,
lacking a curriculum or the resources it needs to function.

While global leaders talk about implementation, the reality is that we should fill in those gaps as youth leaders working with the SDGs and moving between both worlds, where it is not about policy but survival. Back in our home countries, the language is different and questions are not theoretical. Rather, it is a mother choosing between school fees and food; it could be a community leader weighing health and well-being against access, or a student navigating exploitation for grades. Many of these realities do not appear in bullet points or policy briefings, but as youth leaders who share experience with their communities. We represent these realities and carry with us the possibility for change in these high-level spaces. When ground truth validators show up in high-level spaces, they are able to represent the local realities in their rawest form: as urgency, exhaustion, and survival.

Our responsibility to bridge those two worlds is not a glamorous job. It requires our proximity to humanity, to be physically on the ground, working in our various communities so at the end of the day, we can translate a reality we know through our participation, and not through reports, hashtags, or panels. It requires our ability to resist the temptation of downplaying the suffering and struggles of our local communities in order to participate in a diplomatic context. In the architecture of connection, the bridge is not the center of attention; it is where we all hold ourselves accountable and ask ourselves: *Whose reality is being softened? Whose truth is being lost for consensus? What should be done? And who carries the cost when we move on?*

This is where the connection is tested and we must prove humanity as our brand, not the institution. Strangely, this insight did not arrive in a policy room. It arrived on my birthday, while I was dancing, not as a speaker, not as a youth representative, just as a person. That contrast initially unsettled me. I could not help but think: *If our sense of legitimacy disappears the moment we are not performing a role, then what exactly is it built on?*

Institutions are built on the fragile architecture of titles and hierarchies. They require constant maintenance, funding, and permission to survive, while on the other hand, humanity is resilient; it is a self-healing web. When our brand is humanity, we are able to answer the accountability questions and stop trying to represent people and our community from a distance. Instead, we reflect them. We become a mirror of their struggles, and their gut-wrenching realities.

A representative can be replaced by the next person with a title, but a reflection is a shared identity and cannot be replaced or gatekept. When we realize that our survival is a shared resonance effect, the need to protect our little corners of the web disappears. If we fail at recognizing that, the connection fails. We fail at listening to local limitations and weave our local realities into global action.

Our success should be measured by alignment with the improvements of underrepresented and local communities. Global dialogues should be anchored in the schools, farms, clinics, and neighborhoods. Being present in global rooms matters only if those rooms remain tethered to the communities they claim to serve.

Every person we speak to sits in a different place on the web. It could be different cultures, different backgrounds, different vocabularies, and even different emotional states. Choosing simpler words is a way of adapting our communication to the web (the intertwined SDGs) we are weaving for a sustainable world, rather than forcing others to adapt to us. Instead of forcing others to learn and speak in complex jargon, we shift back into the language of our communities and connection.

In 2023, I was invited to be a speaker at the 8th International Youth Conference in collaboration with UNHABITAT, UN Global Communications Civil Society Unit, and AFS Intercultural

Program. I spoke on the topic "Sustainable Solutions: Empowering Youth for a Greener World". During the Q&A segment, a young high school student that travelled all the way from New Jersey to New York asked a question.

He said, "In my school, there's a lot of people who feel scared about where the climate is going and I feel hopeless about the situation of the world seeing the rise in wildfires and global temperatures; and they are afraid to do anything because they feel like they're going to be disappointed. How do we inspire those people to actually start trying to make an effort and improve our world?"

He wasn't asking for a policy paper, he was asking for something to hold onto, a lifeline; a reason for him to wake up every morning without the weight of a dying planet, and most importantly, he was seeking a related example and a practical inspiration. For a split second, like many professional speakers at a conference, I failed to see that during the moment. The professional speaker in me wanted to give him a complex theory, a polished quote about leadership, but that would have been a lie. I knew the answer in my soul, so I was forced to be simple and blunt to match the urgency I saw in his eyes. While I did struggle to answer his question, I started off by explaining to him the difference between an influencer and an advocate.

When you are an influencer, you perform hope for the camera or for people, hence you are disconnected from the problem. But an advocate is a pragmatic firebrand who builds the structure that makes hope possible, inviting others to be part and parcel of that structure. Even if they do not respond, the structure still stands. I told him if he wants hope, he has to be pragmatic. My answer was followed by a case in point of how I started planting staple food from my country when I was encouraging other Sierra Leoneans online to plant their own food, due to the imminent surge of cost of living, leaving many low-income families with barely anything to eat.

A few days after the event he texted me on LinkedIn that he was organizing eco-friendly events at his school. Then I realized two things: firstly, that for years, society has been teaching us how to influence a room instead of weaving reality, which explains why I initially struggled to give him a tangible solution. Secondly, stripping off my professional fluff or jargon created a bridge and gave him the only thing that matters — a starting point. That is the architecture of connection. That is partly how we weave Sustainable Development Goals.

Oftentimes we find ourselves in spaces where complex and heavy words are used, but it hinders growth or progress. If our message is complex, it dies with the person who heard it, because they are afraid of saying it wrong to pass it on. Simple words or messages, on the other hand, have so much impact. It gives others permission to act on the issues they care about whether it is clean water in their community or tackling climate change. It allows a student, or a youth delegate at a conference to repeat it to their friends, who can then repeat it to their parents. And when those messages are backed up by our personal stories, it gives them the blueprint to act.

If back then, someone had come up to me and told me "We need to achieve SDG 4 (Quality Education) or SDG 13 (Climate Action), I would have been perplexed and perhaps jaded. But if they told me, students are being exploited for grades or our environment is being polluted and it is leading to airborne disease and sickness, I would have listened. This is because I witnessed it myself, felt it, and lived it. That is when I stopped being a spectator. The same applies to this young man: if I had used complex or polished words, he would have been wowed but still left with the question "how?"

In a world as complex as global policy or climate change, simplicity is scalability. Information should be light and simple in order to be able to weave across strands effortlessly, reaching everyone in every corner of the web.

The sustainable development goals are often presented as separate goals or issues, but effectively, they are an interconnected web. In many youth spaces, networking has become a performance, a rush to exchange LinkedIn QR codes, to collect contacts, and stand near power without asking what those connections are actually meant to hold.

A sustainable world that embodies that web of SDGs is not built by chance. Institutions do not change simply because they are convinced, neither is networking abstract. Every strand, every individual in these spaces, connects to at least one SDG, whether it is climate action, good health, quality education or gender equality. We are an anchor to strengthen each other and weave into a larger story.

When we gather at youth forums and engagements such as ECOSOC Youth Forum, we are brought into these rooms with intentions to not just network, but to also map. Mapping means understanding who you are connected to, why you are connected, and what that connection is meant to carry. It is the work of ensuring that progress in one area of the SDG does not come at the expense of another.

For example, John may work primarily on SDG 8 which is Decent Work and Economic Growth, while I focus on SDG 10 (Reduced Inequalities). If I am going to network with John, I need to understand not just why John is passionate about SDG 8, but how it is connected to SDG 10; how economic growth without equity deepens inequality, and how inequality undermines sustainable growth. Once we understand this, our strands begin to reinforce each other.

But too often, I have been in rooms where we all talk about collaboration while quietly competing for the same opportunities. We shake each other's hands while measuring proximity. We network, but we do not weave. Youth leadership is not about choosing one SDG to represent. It is about caring enough to hold the entire web, knowing that when one strand fails, partnership becomes impossible.

CHAPTER 3

Moored: Weaving Through Fractured Threads

"It turns out that most of life is just the nothing in the middle" (Obama and Robinson). In a podcast, Michelle Obama uses this idea to emphasize resilience among many things: you keep going, keep building, even when nothing spectacular seems to be happening. From my personal experience as a weaver, I describe this as the in-between season. The gap between the day you realized the world was broken, and the day the world finally gave you the funding or platform to fix it. In this space there are no microphones, no conferences, and no funding. There is only silence.

We often mistake this silence for a lack of progress. We think because nothing is happening means nothing is growing, but this is where we should become moored. In the in-between, to be moored is to refuse to be swept away by the frustration of a fractured system. To be moored is to refuse to let go of the truth even if, or when, global development tells you it does not exist. To be moored is the realization that if the leaders lose their way, we must tighten up the strands regardless of a few broken threads, so the entire structure does not fail — so our world does not fail. To be moored is to be aware that the platform is a tool and not a destination. If you skip being moored in the in-between, you build a structure that collapses the moment the first storm hits.

Michelle Obama's idea of 'nothing in the middle' is the same as Matthew Modine's answer to the question of how to stay steadfast when the vision of global leaders does not align with our reality. Their answer is to keep *weaving*, to keep doing the real work.

As I continue to reflect on both of their words even as I write this chapter, I understand that it is a lesson in structural integrity. Matthew was not talking about protest; he was talking about persistence. For one to keep weaving through conflict and scarcity demonstrates the highest form of local courage needed to create global change. Mrs. Obama was talking about resilience in the quiet. Because in the in-between, we are stripped of our titles as youth ambassador, delegate, or community leader, and we are left with our humanity. And if we can still stand by our vision for a sustainable world when it is corny and unfunded, our legitimacy is no longer built on roles; it is built on our humanity and mooring.

In 2021, I was a television presenter at the Sierra Leone Broadcasting Corporation Youth Zone — a national platform with the power to reach millions where we talked about culture, alleviating poverty, child prostitution, climate change, drug abuse and the rapid dropout of teenagers from school, amongst other issues. As young presenters, we were firebrands. We had the passion to call it as it was, but we were operating in a space owned by the very people we wanted to hold accountable.

When I realized we were not allowed to hold them accountable for certain things, I didn't quit. Rather I teamed up with a colleague of mine and we used the station's credibility as a foundation to build an independent organization which we used to have them maintain responsibility through our presence. We became anchored in local realities — a shift from performative work on television to actual service — spotlighting what it means to be a leader. We started visiting and engaging with underserved schools across the country. Our on-the-ground work became an extension of our TV roles and it was a strategic mooring that allowed us to do the real work.

When I stood on the school grounds in Sierra Leone, one of the things I noticed wasn't a lack of interest, but a lack of infrastructure that no data set was capturing. There was a critical gap between education and agriculture that official data misses. The report usually says 90% of schools have an agricultural curriculum, but they ignore the fact that 0% have seeds or tools. This is an explicit representation of the data-reality gap between the world represented in high-level rooms and the actual world of local reality.

Modine's *"keep weaving"* wasn't a suggestion to ignore the problem; it was more of an instruction on tension. In hindsight, as I stand in the reflection of those school grounds I visited, I now realize I was not just looking at the absence of agricultural materials; I was looking at a failure of imagination. I started asking myself: *How can we as a society shift from reactive approaches to proactive solutions that address root causes rather than symptoms? How can we stay moored through what is already fractured?*

We are often taught and have been trained to celebrate the "action" such as the donation, the ribbon-cutting, or the momentary fix. But my upbringing and on-the-ground work experience gave me a different lens for understanding crises. Growing up in my country Sierra Leone, I was in the habit of arguing with elderly people in my life — something I am not proud of now, but it was one that shaped my ears to hear what they were really saying. While my mom's responses came with slaps that would make you consider packing your bags, my dad and grandma spoke in language of the moored: proverbs and parables. One in particular has stuck with me, playing in my mind like a warning as I look at the 0% agricultural materials in our schools.

Here's the parable that comes to mind:

There was a town that woke up one morning to find a vulture resting in the square. The people were alarmed and drove it away with sticks. When it finally fell, some said, "At least we won." But an elderly woman who was sitting on a stool, lost in her thoughts, replied "Winning is not what troubles me. What troubles me is the luck that brought the vulture here and what luck will follow after."

In global rooms, we are very good at driving away vultures. We write reports about the birds we have chased but we rarely sit on the stool like the elderly woman and ask why the luck of our system keeps bringing the vultures back. To be moored is for us to stop swinging the stick and start changing the luck. It is for us to refuse to celebrate the fall of the vulture without asking what invited it.

To the elderly woman sitting on the stool, the "luck" wasn't a mystery; it was a result of neglected strands. In the context of our work, "luck" is often just a word we use to hide a lack of accountability. When we report that 90% of schools have a curriculum but ignore the 0% that have tools, we are choosing to ignore the luck that brought the vulture. True accountability is not just about counting what we did; it is about being honest about what we failed to provide and holding space for the root causes — a constant, steady presence.

"Participation alone does not change systems. What changes outcomes is sustained, grounded action and willingness to take responsibility when we still have another chance to make better decisions."

— **Corinna Hawkes**, Director, Agrifood Systems and Food Safety Division for the Food and Agriculture Organization of the United Nations

CHAPTER 4

The Weaver's Web: Stories of Local Courage

We often treat the SDGs like separate boxes to be checked, and other times, like a list of seventeen heavy chores handed down from a high-level room; but something new I have learned is that they are a gift. You might be perplexed and wonder why I call it a gift when we all know they can be challenging. Here is how I see it: the gift of the SDGs isn't the goals or targets themselves, rather it's the interconnectedness they reveal. When you pull the strand of Life Below Water, you realize it is tied to Good Health as well as Peace and Justice, and it doesn't stop there. You also discover when you solve a problem at its root, the benefits are distributed in other areas throughout the web of SDGs.

In this chapter you will be seeing powerful stories of changemakers fighting the good fight and impacting their communities — holding the fort while reminding us that you don't need to start with a million dollars in funding. When you are the architect and the tool, you have the capacity to drive change.

One changemaker's story opened my eyes to have a better understanding of seeing the gift of the SDGs. She talked about planting mangroves to sequester carbon, which resonated with different strands of the SDGs. Her willingness and approach to tackling the environmental crisis became so effective that it started uprooting the hopelessness that leads to drug addiction in her community. I sat with this and thought:

"In the old way of thinking, people tried to fix drug use with a lecture, which rarely worked because we were not addressing the 'Bad Luck' of the environment. But when we understand that the SDGs are interconnected – the gift of the SDGs – we are now allowed to be proactive in addressing multiple issues instead of just one". For instance, by confronting the crisis of the Blue Economy, as seen through the work of this changemaker, she was inadvertently bolstering the resources to aid in the resolution of

Peace and Decent Work by empowering young people to act in their communities.

Not everyone has a platform, but many have an impact. Some of the most powerful stories come from people who are not in the spotlight — students, mothers, farmers, teachers, street volunteers, etc. While the world celebrates Malala, how often do we hear about Aissatou— a girl in rural Senegal who teaches others to read by candlelight? We know Greta. But what about Samuel from a village in Gambia, who built a clean water system for his entire community? The world honors the crowned but we must also honor the unseen, brave and quiet changemakers building a better world in silence.

On July 5th, 2025 I posted a public service announcement with a link encouraging young change-makers to submit their stories of impact. In my capacity as a messenger, I intend on building a platform to amplify these stories and inform the world that while global leaders debate solutions, young people are weaving them, even when their efforts are not seen. Included in this chapter, are some of the collections of real and impactful life stories of young changemakers with their permission for inclusion — not just those with titles, but anyone under 30 who is driving impact in their community. From grassroots to global, every action counts. For every young leader feeling imposter syndrome, remember this: *no impact is too small.* You might think you are just teaching a child to swim, or to read by a candle light, but because of the resonance effect, you are actually reinforcing the entire web of their life. Your actions in supporting one goal can reinforce or progress another related goal of well-being in a different area of their life. You are a weaver who has been given a set of 17 tools that all speak to each other. That is the gift, because you are never working on just one thing.

NOTE: You may not see yourself in every place, custom, or every lived reality in these stories because culture shapes us differently; but you will see yourself in the feeling that drives them: the fear, the doubt, the strength, the persistence, and the refusal to give up. Those are human truths, and humanity is the bridge between us.

Mahlet Zeleke Redi

Addis Ababa, Ethiopia

"As a young African woman, I know this truth: privilege is not a crown to wear, it's a tool to build. We rise by making space, by opening doors, and by turning power into purpose."

I'm Mahlet Zeleke Redi, a proud Ethiopian, unapologetic woman advocate, young changemaker, and global youth leader committed to advancing the Sustainable Development Goals. I serve as Executive Director of Women Economic Empowerment Africa and as the Global Focal Point for Decent Jobs and Employment at the UN Major Group for Children and Youth. From grassroots action to high-level global policy spaces, I represent and champion the voices of young people – especially girls – and women working toward a more just, inclusive, and sustainable world. I believe deeply in an Africa that rises by uplifting women and girls first. I began my journey in social impact as early as 6th grade, when I entered a school competition with the intention of doing something meaningful for my community.

That small step planted the seed for everything that followed. While I was in high school, I launched a campaign called "One Book From One Person." My goal was simple: to collect books and school supplies so that no child would be left behind when it came to education. Over the years, I gathered thousands of books and donated them to rural schools, universities, and community libraries. That initiative has now grown into a long-standing program run by the organization I lead, continuing to support public school libraries and ensure equitable access to learning materials for students across Ethiopia.

In university, my perspective deepened. While pursuing my degree in Economics and writing my thesis on the impact of debt sustainability on Ethiopia's economic growth, I started to explore why women's participation in the economy remained so limited. That's when I discovered how period poverty plays a major role in girls dropping out of school, creating long-term impacts on both their futures and national development. I also learned that in some areas, women were still being forced to isolate themselves during menstruation. I couldn't stand by. I wanted to help remove these barriers and create a bridge that supports women to fully engage in both education and economic life. That's how the @icare_power_period campaign was born and During the COVID-19 pandemic, our efforts became even more critical.

Families were facing difficult choices between basic needs and education. We stepped in to support young women with dignity kits and launched partnerships to help girls stay in school. I advocated for reducing the tax on menstrual products in Ethiopia, to make them more affordable for all. We also brought together manufacturers, policymakers, and key stakeholders to create a united approach to menstrual equity. Through strategic partnerships with organizations like Jegnit Ethiopia, Adey Pads, and our own Birqe Dignity Bucket initiative we've reached hundreds of thousands of women and girls in schools, hospitals, prisons, and internally displaced persons (IDP) centers. Birqe plays a vital role by providing reusable menstrual kits and ensuring girls can manage their periods safely and with dignity. These collaborations not only offer immediate support, but also aim to create long-term systems that protect and empower women and girls. Beyond MHM and education, I've expanded my work to focus on economic justice and sustainable development.

Today, I serve as the Global Focal Point for Decent Jobs & Employment at the United Nations Major Group for Children and Youth (UNMGCY), where I represent youth voices in global policy dialogues, particularly around SDG 8 on Decent Work and Economic Growth. In this role, I contribute to UN processes by advocating for youth-inclusive labor policies, skills development, and a just transition to green and digital economies. It has given me the opportunity to speak at major international forums, including the UN General Assembly, and ensure that youth from Africa and the Global South are not only heard—but actively shaping solutions. But my commitment doesn't stop at diplomacy or international policy spaces. I'm also grounded in grassroots action. I'm actively involved in farming and agricultural development, working to create green jobs and promote food security.

I believe sustainable development must be both global and local. Through my work on the ground, I aim to provide young people with real employment opportunities while contributing to climate resilience and nutrition solutions. Creating green, decent jobs in agriculture is not just an economic strategy, it's a social responsibility. To connect and scale all these efforts, I founded Global HER Africa, an initiative operating across multiple African countries. It supports women and youth through leadership development, entrepreneurship, and policy engagement, building ecosystems where they can thrive and lead lasting change.

My story began with a book drive, but today, it's about building ecosystems where girls can stay in school, women can thrive economically, and young people can lead across every sector. My hope is to continue creating inclusive, sustainable, and equitable systems where dignity and opportunity are not just dreams, but lived realities.

The Resonance:

Throughout the course of Mahlet's description of the work she has made throughout the community, we see efforts towards specific SDGs, like SDG 2 (Zero Hunger), SDG 4 (Quality Education), SDG 5 (Gender Equality), and SDG 8 (Decent Work and Economic Growth). However, as we've discussed, efforts in maintaining one strand have an effect on other strands of the web as well, reinforcing development towards other SDGs.

Mahlet noticed that there were children in her community that were ready to learn, but were held back from doing so by poverty. In order to address this, she launched her 'One Book from One Person' campaign, which developed into an institutionalized and sustained program.Throughout the course of her efforts, she made progress in her sector of the community towards SDG 4 (Quality Education).

As Mahlet progressed throughout her education, she noticed how women's lives in her community were being disrupted by the natural process of menstruation. In her approach to target this, she founded the @icare_power_period campaign, eventually partnering with other organizations to bolster her efforts. The work paid off and its effects improved the dignity of women, increased school attendance and health outcomes, while also increasing menstrual equity awareness. This work strongly contributed to the progress in attaining SDG 5 (Gender Equality).

A significant portion of Mahlet's focus has been directed towards how to make structural progress for future conditions. She noticed barriers in how the voices of the youth were locked out of policy rooms, and how women as a whole had been effectively locked out of becoming powerful agents in the economy. In order to combat this, she actively uses her platform to advocate for labor-inclusive policies involving youth and women. These actions have produced and contributed to the influence of the policy framework regarding decent work and a greener economy, aligning with SDG 8 (Decent Work and Economic Growth). In her work towards SDG 8, we see how it is inextricably linked with her focus on bettering the climate and creating a more sustainable future, aiding in SDG 13 (Climate Action).

Throughout the course of her journey, Mahlet worked in several domains of the SDGs. With her experience and understanding that no singular system alone can completely dismantle systemic inequality, she founded the initiative of Global HER Africa, demonstrating partnership on progress towards the different domains of the SDGs, and also explicitly focusing on SDG 17 (Partnership for the Goals).

Mahlet's story reminded me of our shared humanity—especially the gut-wrenching feeling when you realize something is wrong in your community. From her story, we see how one gut-wrenching feeling acted upon can affect other sustainable development goals. It is also a case in point to the presence of the reality gap in our communities which is often ignored. What stood out most is her ability to turn awareness into tangible action, holding people accountable through her presence and bringing institutions together. Her ground work became the catalyst that enabled her to connect multiple SDGS, showing how agriculture, education, and gender equality are interconnected in achieving food security and economic justice.

Kisimir Sanguyan Saibulu

Nairobi, Kenya

"No idea is too small to bring change. We are others' burden-admire to lead and advocate for change."

I stood on the parched earth of Amboseli, the stench of death rising from the carcasses of Maasai livestock. Over 80% gone in the 2022 drought, the backbone of my people's livelihood shattered. Women, already sidelined, faced an impossible burden as men traveled far in desperate searches for water and pasture.

Motivated by their struggle, myself and a small group of young Maasai elites dared to dream bigger. We initiated Amboseli Wildlife and Communities, focusing directly on the Maasai women. Illiteracy, extreme poverty, and no reliable funding loomed as deep challenges. Yet, fueled by the resilience of our community, we refused to look away. Our radical idea: empower these women through sustainable poultry farming, ecosystem restoration, and scholarships for young girls.

Today, over sixty women, once burdened, nurture thriving chicken coops and cultivate green gardens. They have found the dignity of earning a living, transforming their homes and futures. This is our story of hope, an ongoing adventure unfolding for a tomorrow where every woman has a voice, and people and wildlife coexist in harmony.

The Resonance:

Kisimir's narrative, though concise, phenomenally demonstrates the interwoven structure of the web through his action towards supporting his community. In facing the collapse of food resources and resulting economic challenges posed to the community due to the drought, Kisimir produced a multidimensional solution that aids in the amelioration of conditions that several of the SDGs target.

He noticed how women in his community were experiencing the crisis equally, though they were not equipped with the power or ability to take action towards it. Kisimir's inspiration turned his focus to empowering the abilities of this group, strengthening the strands in his web. He initiated literacy programs and child girl scholarships to develop opportunities for them to be more involved in spaces where solutions are created, and to create solutions themselves. This involves both SDG 4 (Quality Education), SDG 5 (Gender Equality), and SDG 8 (Decent Work and Economic Growth).

In addition to this, Kisimir and the women of his community turned their efforts towards sustainable poultry farming and ecosystem restoration through gardening. This enters into the domains of SDG 8 (Decent Work and Economic Growth), SDG 11 (Sustainable Cities and Communities, and SDG 15 (Life on Land).

As noted, progress in one SDG is intertwined with progress in other SDGs. The multidimensional solution created by Kisimir also explicitly demonstrates SDG 17 (Partnership for the Goals).

Kisimir's story is one of those poignant narratives that stays with you because of its vivid reminder that hope is local. This story shows how deeply intertwined the SDGs are and crucial for survival, even in the least places you might expect, like Amboseli village. In the face of drought, loss, and marginalization, they do not wait for the solutions to be handed to them. They fought for hope. SDGs are not just global goals but practical lifelines for survival, dignity, and coexistence, especially in communities that are overlooked. Meanwhile the impacts of climate change are already a crucial aspect of their reality.

Roseline Adewuyi

Oyo, Nigeria

"Empower a girl, and you ignite a ripple of change that transforms communities and shapes the future."

I am Roseline Adewuyi, and my journey as a gender advocate began long before I even had the words to describe it. Growing up in Nigeria, I became acutely aware of how leadership was subtly and sometimes overtly presented as something girls should not aspire to. From classrooms to school clubs, I saw how boys were readily encouraged to lead, while girls were often relegated to supporting roles.

This early exposure to gender bias planted the seeds of my advocacy. Even in higher institutions, places that should be hallmarks of enlightenment and intellectual freedom, I noticed how leadership opportunities were often gatekept by outdated stereotypes. Girls who dared to lead were met with resistance, questioned for their ambition, or made to feel out of place. I found myself constantly wondering: how can institutions meant to promote critical thinking and progress reinforce such limiting beliefs about what girls can and cannot do? These experiences were not just observations; they were deeply personal.

As a student who chose to pursue the arts, particularly French, in a context where brilliance was often equated with science and technology, I had to push against the grain. I did not let it stop me. Instead, it fueled my determination to challenge these norms and create spaces where girls could not only dream but also lead and thrive. This is what birthed my advocacy. It came from a desire to dismantle the internalized and institutionalized gender stereotypes that hold girls back, especially in educational spaces.

I started the Roseline Initiative, organizing mentorship programs, leadership seminars, and gender advocacy campaigns, particularly targeting secondary schools. I wanted to intervene early to help girls see that leadership is not reserved for boys and to help boys unlearn toxic beliefs about gender roles. It has not always been easy. There have been moments of pushback, moments of isolation, and moments of doubt. What kept me going was the change I started to see.

Girls began speaking up, stepping forward, and believing in their own voices. The joy of watching a timid girl grow into a confident leader or seeing a school club embrace inclusive leadership gave me the motivation to keep pushing. The impact has been humbling. My work has reached thousands of young people across Nigeria, helping them rethink gender roles and empowering girls to pursue leadership boldly.

I have been privileged to share my message on global platforms, but what matters most to me is the local change. That shift in mindset begins in classrooms and extends into communities. My dream is clear. I envision a future where no girl feels she has to shrink herself to be accepted. A future where educational institutions actively challenge and remove gender stereotypes, rather than reinforce them. A future where girls grow up knowing that leadership is not exclusive to any gender, but a reflection of human potential. That is the future I am working toward, one empowered girl at a time.

Roseline's actions clearly demonstrate progress in supporting gender equality (SDG 8). This grew out of a need she saw presented to her in her community, over and over again, with fellow girls and women relegated to the side and not given the opportunity to be in places of power. When we dive deeper into how Roseline took action in promoting gender equality, we see that the steps she took did not just exist in the domain of SDG 5, but were also present in SDG 4 (Quality Education), and SDG 10 (Reduced Inequalities).

In order to promote gender equality and support the women in her community, Roseline focused on dismantling systemic issues that shape ways of thinking. Not only did she take the time to educate boys in her community in unlearning toxic beliefs and supporting the rights of others, she focused efforts into supporting young women and equipping them with the beliefs and skills to seize potential future opportunities for leadership.

In addition to sharing her story and demonstrating the interwoven nature of the action in undertaking the SDGs, Roseline illustrates the concept of 'moored'. She shares, in part, about how the road in her quest has not always been without obstacles, and how there has been pushback – nevertheless she persisted. Whether that be in demonstrating how intelligence can exist in the humanities, just as it may exist in sciences and technologies; or in refusing to abandon the support she and her team created for young women in her community. That is being moored.

Rosaline's story reveals a truth many of us have felt: gatekeeping. In her case it goes deeper beyond any anecdotal criticism as a youth ambassador, because she has additional challenges posed to her as a woman. It shows how gender barriers can limit progress. Even in higher institutions where we expect progress and the scale to be balanced, outdated beliefs still shape who gets to lead. Her story is a reminder that gender bias runs deeper than everyday sexism and it's happening now, everywhere—in classrooms, clubs, and institutions. What inspires me most is her commitment to creating spaces where girls can lead through mentorship and inclusivity to ensure education becomes a platform for empowerment rather than limitation.

Rita Awesti John

Mombasa, Kenya

"We are not waiting to lead tomorrow; we are already rising today with courage in our hearts and change in our hands."

I'm Rita Awesti, a youth leader, feminist and community organizer from Mombasa, Kenya. Growing up on the coast, I witnessed how climate change, drug abuse, youth unemployment and gender inequality intersected to harm my peers and environment. These challenges inspired me to act, not just by responding to problems, but by building solutions from the ground up. I founded and led the Shark Swimming Club, a social enterprise which trains youths in swimming, water safety and lifeguard skills. For many of our participants, especially those from informal settlements and underserved schools, it's their first time learning to swim, a skill that not only prevents drowning but builds confidence, discipline and new career pathways in the blue economy. As of today, we've trained over 100 youths in water safety and swimming, with 20 progressing into advanced courses and lifeguard certification. Beyond the skills, our programs have reduced risky behaviors like drug use and idleness by offering youths meaningful alternatives and positive role models. Alongside this, I co-lead Step Up Pandya, a youth-led initiative focused on waste management, recycling and environmental conservation.

We've mobilized over 1000 community members for beach clean-ups, facilitated environmental education in local schools, community barazas and planted more than 600 mangrove trees. Young people who once viewed waste as useless now see opportunity, turning plastic into income and pride. We've seen women starting small eco-enterprises and youths forming green clubs to continue advocacy in their schools and neighborhoods. Through my training with Collaboration of Women in Development (CWID), Akili Dada and other partners, I became a Health Champion. I now lead SRHR (Sexual and Reproductive Health and Rights) and SGBV (Sexual and Gender-Based Violence) conversations in public health facilities and grassroots community spaces. These forums have helped women and girls understand their rights, access health services without shame and speak up against violence. Several survivors have come forward to seek help, and healing and some have even become peer mentors themselves.

My feminist journey deepened through Akili Dada's movement-building program, where I connected with other young African women who are transforming systems. As an Akili Dada Blue Economy Ambassador for Coastal Kenya, I bridge marine-related economic opportunities with grassroots youths, creating awareness and facilitating enrollment into vocational programs like KBEST at Mombasa Polytechnic and Kisauni Vocational Training Centre. This has led to more young people, especially girls, seeing themselves as future marine biologists, conservationists or maritime workers. I also serve on the Nyali District Peace Committee, where I co-organize youth peace dialogues in Kadzandani, Nyali sub-county and engage in annual Peace Walks, engaging more than 500 youths in discussions on conflict resolution, security and civic responsibility. These efforts have built stronger relationships between local leadership and the youths as well as reducing tension in hotspot areas.

Despite challenges — like limited funding, burnout and community resistance — what keeps me going is the visible change: that woman and the girl who now speaks with confidence, the youth who chose mentorship over drug addiction, the cleaner beaches, the restored mangroves, the communities coming together in hope. My dream is to replicate these models across the region and continent, building a youth-led, community-driven ecosystem where justice, sustainability and empowerment are not just ideals, but realities. I believe young people are not just beneficiaries of change. We are the architects of a better world.

The Resonance:

Rita's story demonstrated a wonderful combination of communal empathy, determination, and unity. Her efforts in tandem with those around her connect to a numerous SDGs, whether that be through their environmental impact, her focus on health disparities, career access, or supporting local youth.

Her narrative begins with a clear focus on SDG 13 (Climate Action), SDG 14 (Life Below Water), and SDG 15 (Life on Land). This is seen most explicitly through her involvement in *Step Up Pandya*, where she organized beach clean ups and planting mangrove trees. These SDGs are also supported in her efforts towards SDG 4 (Quality Education), SDG 11 (Sustainable Cities and Communities), and SDG 12 (Responsible Consumption and Production). In addition to her co-leadership of *Step Up Pandya*, she also started and led the *Shark Swimming Club* which focused on the educational element behind environmental and ecological growth. These efforts correlated with her work at *KBEST* to show support for SDG 8 (Decent Work and Economic Growth) through providing education and vocation opportunities to youth.

As we have observed throughout the course of our analysis of these narratives, the SDGs are often inseparable. Progress in one domain affects the progress in another. In her work with the youth of her communities, she had an impact on SDG 3 (Good Health and Well-Being), through providing alternative opportunities that prevented drug use amongst youth. Her efforts were compounded in this domain through her work with the *Collaboration of Women in Development (CWID)*, and Akili Dada, allowing her to lead conversations in sexual reproductive health and rights, as well as gender-violence. This work connects her efforts in SDG 3 to the domain of SDG 5 (Gender Equality) and SDG 10 (Reduced Inequalities).

Beyond this, Rita demonstrates profound support in the accomplishment of SDG 16 (Peace, Justice and Strong Institutions), and SDG 17 (Partnership for the Goals). This is seen in her work with Nyali Peace District Committee, where she organizes peace walks, and engages young members of the community so they are responsible in forming important civic foundations for themselves going forward.

Rita's work in Mombasa reveals a secret of the web. When she took the responsibility to teach young men to swim and plant mangroves, she was not just addressing SDG 14 (Life Below); rather she was also re-weaving their sense of worth. An environmental task inadvertently cured the idleness and drug use that the "Map" treats as separate issues. This is the resonance effect—when a proactive solution for one root causes vibrations across the entire community, fixing symptoms we did not even initially set out to touch. This is a gift of the SDGs.

Godwin Kevin

Vietnam

"Change begins when you find what is most important to you."

My name is Godwin Kevin, I come from Nigeria and currently I am a full-time undergraduate student at Vin University. In my free time, I am a competitive debater and part of the debate club at my university. I love to read about history, economics, human psychology and international relations and politics. My realm is the social sciences. Aside from all these, I consider myself a changemaker; here is my story:

Coming from a country with over 200 million people, 60% of which are youth, one would think that with such a young workforce, the youth would be most actively involved in key issues and decision making in the country, however that isn't quite the case. Far too many aren't even given opportunities or platforms to speak and share their ideas, instead they follow societal norms and remain not having been thought of or allowed to defy the status quo to let their voices be heard. There's barely room for young people to think outside the box, develop their talents and skills, or build their ideas.

In 2018 I volunteered for an organization in my city. We would go to schools to organize seminars and workshops. During a session that I hosted, I asked the students to tell me about entrepreneurship. After waiting for minutes, the hall was quiet and the students looked confused. Nobody could give me an answer; it was saddening, because in a 'standard' school with a population of over 500 students, not even its prefects could answer or define what entrepreneurship meant. To think these students are groomed to become leaders in our society but are lacking the base or adequate knowledge on what drives innovation and massive change all over the world. After the seminar, I saw this as a huge missed opportunity, not just for my country but for the world at large.

Having had access to norm defying teenagers like Godwin Egba, James Okina, Mirabelle Morah, amongst others, I knew firsthand how much difference it would make in our societies to have more teenagers and leaders like them. I was determined to help these teenagers access life changing opportunities through mentorship and interactive seminars. That idea morphed into and birthed what I now lead as "Inspire for Greatness". Inspire for Greatness is a youth-led nonprofit organization that empowers young people, while equipping them with resources they need to reach their greatest potential and become global citizens. Inspire for Greatness is a safe space where young people can share their ideas, develop talents, and defy stereotypes.

Through my initiative, I have helped bridge the gap between talent and opportunity by providing over 3,000+ young people from 15 African countries with self-development programs to cultivate their entrepreneurial and leadership skills, while also fostering collaboration and partnerships with the United Nations' sustainability goals. For example, Inspire for Greatness has organized virtual and onsite mentorship programs across Africa. These mentorship programs have empowered young people to build healthy self-esteem and inspired them to take the first steps to becoming changemakers in their respective communities. By leveraging my network, I have made these opportunities and resources accessible to young people throughout Africa. At present, Inspire for Greatness has 15 volunteer team members and

30 mentors who support the initiative's work across operations, finance, and videography. I named my project 'Inspire for Greatness' so anytime I hear the name, I am reminded of my mission, the journey I have embarked on and each and every day my vision becomes clearer to me.

The Resonance:

Throughout Godwin's narrative, we learn that his primary objective is to focus closely on the skills and education that youth are equipped with for business and entrepreneurship. This need grew out of what he saw in his community, the opportunity he had been graced with through his relationships with others, and a desire to impart that opportunity on others in order to create a more hopeful and prosperous community in his future.

Godwin set out to accomplish a long term goal in educating future entrepreneurs and ensuring that they have a strong foundation from which they can act on in the future. This long term goal situates itself in the domains of SDGs 8 (Decent Work and Economic Growth), and 9 (Industry, Innovation and Infrastructure). However, the method through which he goes about achieving it is effectively strengthening the level of education that the youth are receiving, existing in the domain of SDG 4 (Quality Education).

Through his efforts, Godwin is explicitly tackling the issue of misrepresentation, stating how that majority of the population consists of youth, yet they are not equipped with the ability or means of full agency; this resolves tensions in inequality and thus connects to SDG 10 (Reduced Inequalities). Apart from this, Godwin's engagement with the youth is inadvertently occupying them with positive structure, a sense of dignity, and future directed goals, preventing them from engaging in high-risk behaviors, and forming a sense of collaboration and engagement with the different pillars of their community – indirectly corresponding to SDGs 1 (No Poverty), 3 (Good Health), and 17 (Partnership for the Goals).

Godwin's story is a profound case in point of the weaver identifying a structural silence. Looking at the resonance here—found in the transition from a quiet hall to a continental network— should remind us of the "0% tools" I talked about in the Moored chapter. When Godwin stood before 500 students who could not define their own agency, he performed an accidental audit. He then realized that without the language of entrepreneurship and permission to defy norms, these students were built as a fragile institution designed to fit into existing boxes, rather than resilient humans capable of building their own.

His work shows us that when you find a room where the truth is being softened by a lack of tools, our job as a weaver is to provide the vocabulary and opportunities for change and not let the silence stay in the room.

Arthurlina Johnson

Freetown, Sierra Leone

"Women and girls are not back benchers; we are warriors and not worriers. We are the jewels of society and we play an important role in human capital development."

Growing up, I've witnessed how a woman's life has been defined by society: who they become, what they do, and their role. I've always believed that women should have equal rights to choose or decide their lives just as men do. If God could give everyone the freedom to choose, who are those that want to decide what women should do and not do? I have always spoken up for my friends who have been treated badly by their dating partner, and reminded them of their worth and right as a human to do better or be treated better.

Two major things inspired me to start up an organization to empower girls with every opportunity available, especially skills they could learn. One of which was my mom. I grew up in a home where my dad abandoned us at the arrival of the fourth child (the last born of my family). My mom was left with the responsibility of the home, including taking care of our schooling. It was a rough phase for her. She became selfless, and focused on us.

I asked myself, *if my mom wasn't educated, and employed, would she have been able to take care of us?* That struck me, and led me to the realization that women deserved quality education and jobs just as much as men. We never suffered for what to eat, wear, or where to sleep, because my mom was educated and working. It wasn't easy, but she survived and thrived.

So I thought to myself, *many women will do better for themselves and kids if they are given the equal opportunity that men receive.* I decided to start raising awareness within my little corner that, "education is the only husband that will not divorce women."

Another key inspiration was my first year in the university. I observed that the ladies are so apathetic to read and do their academic work themselves. They rely on the gents to do their work for them, while they 'slay and stay pretty' in class. I was so sick and tired of seeing that. So, I decided to reach out to the few that I was able to impact, telling them to do their academic work themselves, and letting them know about the dignity that comes with it. I became the change I want to see. I did my assignments myself, competed with men to actively participate in class discussions during lectures, studied hard to do my presentation perfectly. As a result, my grades were the bomb.

My fellow ladies were moved by my actions and they too started doing the same, studying, participating in class, and performing well in exams. All these inspired me to start up an organization, mainly to create self-awareness among women and girls, boosting their self-esteem and changing the societal norms they have been taught about themselves.

I'm still working on impacting more women and girls, raising awareness for the need for quality education, and skill empowerment. Skill empowerment is a driving force for a better and brighter future. Skills can do what formal education can't. Skills can serve as a side hustle or double income. With women at the center of skill and entrepreneurship, the rate of poverty will drastically reduce.

One of the challenges I faced was to get people to believe in what I stand for. Changing a long-standing societal norm about women is no child's play. I met some who argued with me over my dream of raising awareness. Some say I'm wasting my time; the world is an already male dominated place.

The other challenge I encountered was raising funds to organize my first seminar for girls. I only had my mom by my side. She funded the first seminar which targeted girls between the ages 11-21. The turnout of people was not so great. My mom and I were the speakers of the seminar. My mom spoke on the topic, "education is the only husband that will not divorce you," and I spoke on the purpose, and dream of my organization. What kept me going was the urge to do more. I knew I hadn't done enough, there is more to be done, more girls to reach, more lives to transform, and loud voices to make. I did another seminar, which focused on addressing men (who are the perpetrators of what women go through), and skill empowerment. The topics were, "too precious to be defiled," and "skill empowerment."

My seminars impacted school pupils who attended the second seminar. I had a lot of feedback after the second seminar. To this day, people are reaching out, asking for more seminars to be organized. This is just the beginning for my organization. I have a lot in mind that I want to do, when the right funding and sponsors show face. I plan on organizing more of those seminars as well as training on skills like: fashion design, cake baking, decoration and many more. I want to see a society where women and girls know who they are, what they want, and who they want to become.

The Resonance:

Arthulina's story demonstrates the very poignant reality of women around the world, particularly in Sierra Leone: that of existing in a society which disempowers women and unconsciously educates them to believe that they are secondary and dependent upon men for survival. Arthurlina had to face this reality in her personal life through the experience she faced with her family and her friendships. She saw the need in her community and within her life, so she began to do what she could in order to resolve the tension of gender inequality and patriarchy; this is a clear and explicit effort made in the domain of SDG 5 (Gender Inequality).

Arthulina began by aiming her efforts towards her peers based on her observations. She used her influence and passion to shift other women in her community from a passive and potentially dependent perspective to one of agency and empowerment through the development of skills. Through these skills, women are equipped with the means to accomplish what they desire and also the agency to self-determine, supplying them with a greater foundation of dignity and self-respect.

Her efforts began to focus further on female empowerment and skill development through her seminars. In these seminars, she stresses the importance of education in youth, teaching them that if they invest in themselves, they are ensured safety and security in the future. These seminars also address the patriarchy existing in society for women, preparing them with the tools they need to go forward and prosper. Arthulina understands that this is a group effort, and also provides educational resources for men in hopes to dismantle sources and other impactful dynamics within the patriarchal structure. Her seminars and workshops in skill development are clear efforts in the domain of SDG 4 (Quality Education), and SDG 8 (Decent Work and Economic Growth).

After reading Arthurlina's story, initially I thought the resonance started with the first seminar but after contemplating on it, I realized that it started with the mother's resilience when the father abandoned them. The mother proved that Education is not just a certificate; it is a safety net.

In our global rooms, we talk about women's empowerment as a policy but for this weaver, it was a matter of survival. The mother's life was the audit that proved the daughter's mission. When they stood together on that stage, they were showing the next generation of young girls how to build a life that doesn't crumble even when the main support leaves.

EasySTEM

Freetown, Sierra Leone

"If you're reading this and wondering if your idea matters, if your village is too far, or if you're too young or too unknown, remember so were we."

Lovetta Bangura, Abdul Rahim Jalloh, and Emmanuel Kamanda are the founders of Easy STEM. Lovetta's education was not guaranteed after her father died. She hawked ginger beer on the street of Freetown to make ends meet and to support her education. Rahim grew up curious about technology from tinkering with tools to excelling in robotics. And Emmanuel who lost both parents at a young age experienced instability but overcame and excelled academically with the support of scholarships. It began with one exam night and a simple frustration: no internet to access learning materials. As college students from a low-income family, that moment became the trigger. After conducting research, we discovered that the challenge wasn't just ours—it was nationwide. That discovery sparked a bold idea to make quality education accessible to every child, even without the internet.

Determined to change the narrative, we began brainstorming. With Abdul and Emmanuel's deep technical skills, and Lovetta's energy and vision, we started exploring offline connectivity solutions. Our idea was a portable, offline digital library to provide access to quality online educational and STEM learning material. At first, we called it E-Lab (electronics library).

In 2022, we entered the Generation Unlimited Innovation Challenge as team Lorem. Locally, we competed against other teams across Sierra Leone and won, validating our idea and motivating us to refine the solution. Early on, the team had built a prototype server out of cardboard. It wasn't polished, but it demonstrated the potential and students could access lessons and simulations even without the internet. After the local victory, we redesigned the server with a 3D-printed case, making it durable, portable, and ready for real-world use.

The local success opened the door to the global stage, where we competed among over 10,000 applicants worldwide; we were recognized as one of the Top 10 innovative ideas globally. This achievement reinforced our mission to bring offline digital learning to students everywhere. Following the global recognition, we launched the Tasso Island pilot, deploying the improved server in schools and community centers. Students engaged with interactive lessons, explored simulations, and discovered a new sense of possibility. The server was no longer just a prototype, it was a transformative learning tool, ready to scale.

From our first concept grew Easy STEM, a movement determined to make digital learning accessible to every child. Our innovations include Easy STEM Server (E-Lab) – an offline digital library preloaded with interactive content, simulations, and exam resources. We also developed Digital Learning Hub in a Bag after taking lessons from pilots and student feedback. Our Digital Learning Hub in a Bag, became a portable solar powered backpack that transforms any space into a digital classroom in an instant with tablets, a solar-powered station, a projector, and the EasySTEM Server. So anywhere could become a learning space: a school, a community hall, or even a village center. Lastly, was our Sensebod: an AI-powered personalized learning platform. Sensebod provided lessons, peer learning, real-time feedback, and interactive exercises for students with internet access. By combining mobility with adaptive technology, Easy STEM bridged the gap between offline and online learning.

Where others saw challenges like no Wi-Fi, no electricity, and no infrastructure, we saw possibility. Our mission is to ensure no child is left behind in this digital age, as many students in underserved communities lack access to important resources. So far, our solutions have transformed communities across Sierra Leone. Students in villages who had never touched a tablet are now competing and winning in national and international competitions.

Our belief in partnership to foster Quality Education propelled us to collaborate with African Centre of Technology Studies (ACTS) to develop Sensebod. Because of this collaboration and consistent engagement across diverse classrooms, we have cemented the platform as a central part of Sierra Leone's evolving digital learning ecosystem. We also partnered with the Peace Corps Pilot, and with their support, volunteers were deployed in remote communities to train teachers and students, ensuring the hubs were fully integrated into learning. The pilot revealed the transformative power of hands-on support combined with technology: students thrived and teachers felt empowered rather than abandoned.

Through our work 6,000+ students across the 16 districts in Sierra Leone have gained access to quality education once thought impossible.

The Resonance:

Throughout the evolution of EasySTEM we see a remarkable demonstration of innovation, collaboration, and the state of moored. It began from a personal, local need experienced by Lovetta, Abdul, and Emmanuel, which then transformed into a national source of educational aid and opportunities that transcend local lives into international spaces of competition and opportunity. Despite hardships in their pasts, in their education, and throughout the course of the development of the project, the three creators of EasySTEM persisted into the creation of a product that offers astonishing opportunity to those who had no means of acquiring it through prior means.

Through the development of EasySTEM's *E-Lab*, *Digital Learning Hub in a Bag*, and *Sensebod* they are giving students throughout Sierra Leone the content and tools to access educational resources and aid. This is a clear effort and step in the progress of SDG 4 (Quality Education). In doing so, EasySTEM is indirectly bolstering SDG 8 (Decent Work and Economic Growth) through the support of students in becoming educated and career-ready individuals, as well as SDG 9 (Industry, Innovation and Infrastructure) through their creative and universally applicable educational tools.

Apart from their deliberate work in the domain of education, EasySTEM has made intentional efforts in connecting with other organizations in order to collaborate on goals that extend efforts even further, demonstrating progress in SDG 17 (Partnership for the Goals). Through their work with African Centre of Technology Studies (ACTS), Peace Corps Pilot, and the schools of Sierra Leone, Lovetta, Abdul and Emmanuel have directly impacted the lives and futures of over 6,000 children in Sierra Leone.

Suzanna Raven Schofield

Maryland, United States

"We must dare to hope. And fight until those hopes become reality."

When I was younger, I used to jump off my playhouse that my father and grandmother had built for me and my sister onto the trampoline below. It scared my parents and any friends I had invited over to play, but it was the closest I felt to flying. I wanted my life to be full of moments where I took the world by storm –– living every day to its absolute fullest. Where I jump into the unknown. With danger always lurking in the shadows, I wanted my future to be filled with risks and chances where I said yes and didn't let fear control me. I would fly or spend every single day jumping until I found a way to soar. Funny how life works sometimes. You can try to fly all you want, but Earth's gravity will do everything in its power to pull you down. My gravity story truly began when I was eleven.

Up to when I was seven, I lived in the southern suburbs of Seattle. In November 2008, I moved to Maryland when my dad was transferred to a position at the Social Security headquarters in Baltimore. We moved to Carroll County; a rural area located thirty miles outside of the city. It's predominantly white, conservative, and where I was living, most people were middle class. It was a stark change from the diverse low-income town I lived in on the west coast. Cultural differences included more proper greetings to parents or better clothes, and I felt out of place. 17 years later, I still do. Though, I also no longer fit in with my West Coast community either.

Making friends was strange, and so I grew closer to my sister. We were best friends. We played with toys, would spend countless hours exploring outside, and I would help take care of her while my parents were working. It was engrained into me that it was my biggest duty in life to take care of her. Even despite our dramatic differences — she was caught in fantasy, and me in science — our love for nature is what kept our personalities connected. She would find doors to mermaid coves, or see how the leaves would change color from the fairies that would visit the forests at night, and I would remark on how the plate tectonics shifted Earth and how that impacted the evolution of animals nearby. In each of our own ways, we would find the magic of the environment together.

Things took a turn in the fall of 2012. There is an endemic of Lyme Disease in Maryland. Growing up, playing goalie and center mid-field in soccer, living in the woods, having dogs — these are all conditions that made me prone to getting bit by the ticks that have infiltrated my community due to the overpopulation of deer. Though the disease is sometimes indicated by a bullseye rash, I didn't experience such a response. What I instead experienced was extreme fatigue, pain, and feeling completely not myself. Coming from the West Coast, my family did not recognize the symptoms. Perhaps if we had come from the East Coast, the symptoms would have been easier to catch. By the time we had caught on that something was wrong, Lyme Disease had already taken root in my body.

I would proceed with a heavy dose of antibiotics. These antibiotics would further destroy my immune system. For over ten years, I have faced chronic illness, autoimmune responses, an increase in food sensitivities and allergies, and extreme fatigue and pain. Days became about survival and perseverance. I still had ambitious goals. I wanted to change the world, but it was a struggle to get out of bed in the morning. Activities that would best prepare me for the career I wanted to build now took significant energy and willpower. And, with extreme pain also came a significant impact on my mental health. I was diagnosed with major depressive disorder and anxiety disorder as a freshman in high school. While I was dealing with my own battles, my sister was too. During fall of 2012, when I was taking a rigorous course of antibiotics, my little sister was experiencing the first symptoms of juvenile fibromyalgia.

By the following spring, I remember her pain being so great that she would need to use wheelchairs during school field trips. Her nervous system kept misfiring throughout our childhoods, even to this day. Many diagnoses and many, many years of hospital visits later, she has been diagnosed with several psychological diagnoses including early onset schizophrenia, autism, ADHD, and epilepsy. The true state of everything she deals with is unknown. Her case remains a mystery to the doctors. Every day of my teen years, I watched her live through torture.

For her survival, my family began focusing on her care. What this meant was multiple summers where I spent time alone at home while my mother, father, and sister went into Baltimore to seek relief from medical teams at Shepard Pratt, Johns Hopkins, the University of Maryland, and more. Loneliness and independence became companions of mine. I began pouring myself even more into things that would help people. I started a community garden and founded the Environmental Club at my high school, began a wreath-laying event at a cemetery near the mental hospital in my town, tutored other students, and worked on a range of different advocacy issues. If I couldn't help my sister, I was going to dedicate my life to helping everyone else as much as possible.

Pain takes its toll though, even when you try to avoid it. I knew that I couldn't ever be free to find myself if my life was controlled by the grief and anguish around me. I pursued opportunities far away from home. For two summers in high school, I worked as an Enrollee and then Youth Leader for the Youth Conservation Corps of America in Yellowstone National Park. During a gap year, I worked as a farmhand on a sheep and dairy pastoral in northern Victoria, Australia, as an au pair outside of Brisbane, and as a volunteer at the Australia Zoo in Beerwah. I then attended Wellesley College in Boston. I was a cross-registered student at MIT, studied abroad in England and Kenya, interned in Paraguay, and was part of many student organizations all working to make change. My favorite organization was EnAct which is where I met my life partner, reinstated the Office of Sustainability at my school, conducted fundraisers for issues like food justice and sustainable fashion, and led countless events working to build community while making an impact.

When I graduated in 2024, I joined the Harris-Walz coordinated campaign in Wisconsin where I served as a field organizer in Dane County. After that position, I have continued my work for a water conservation organization and have volunteered for nonprofits focused on issues such as wildlife conservation or public health. I am also working to establish my own nonprofit looking at how we can support community organizations to address issues with a One Health mind frame. One Health applies systems-based approaches to public health and conservation issues. Still, to me, the biggest challenge in my life has been the health and well-being of my sister. While at college, her case got more complicated when she had her first seizure in spring 2022. I spent that summer at home taking care of her as she recovered.

After the election in 2024, I also returned home to take care of her while my family balanced the aftermath of how each person's respective field was defunded. My little sister is still the greatest mystery. And the torment of her mind continues. Every day, she battles some of the worst things I have ever known while still pursuing her dreams. In spring of 2025, she graduated with an Associate of Arts in Dance from Howard Community College. Some doctors told her when she was in middle school that she would never be able to graduate high school, let alone college. Other doctors told her that she would never be able to dance. Again, when you fly, there are so many things that try to bring you back to the ground.

Similar limitations have been told to me. Many of my advisers, teachers, and professors have told me the same sorts of things - that my dreams are too big. That I should strive for something less. That I should hold back because of my health challenges. Working to change the world is hard. Even harder when people don't believe in you. That's why it's good to be a strong, stubborn young woman who doesn't take no for an answer. I know that the systems that are in place right now are wrong. The world is burning around us — political instability, climate change, disease, genocide. The systems will not improve if we do not dare to dream of a better future. And a better future requires better systems. So, we must continue to soar, no matter what the weights are that pull us down.

And what does that jumping and soaring look like in my life so far? I have attended and spoken at UN conferences, won international awards, and went to some of the best schools in the world. I will be attending the University of Oxford to pursue a Master of Science in Biodiversity, Conservation, and Nature Recovery starting Fall 2025. I published my first poetry book *Struck by Lightning: Part 1 of Breaking Sea Glass* with plans to publish more. I run multiple Instagram accounts including one that makes memes to bring awareness, community, and humor to what it means to be a caregiver. I am conducting research in New Zealand on blue carbon futures. I am writing a curriculum on how to increase organizing capacity within the wildlife conservation space. And I do my best to check in with the people I love as a fight against the loneliness and grief that so many of us are feeling.

At the end of the day, in all of the work, the sweat poured, the tears cried — I am still fighting for my sister and for the things she cares about. The world is in a flux of chaos and conflict right now. Fascism and authoritarianism are on the rise. My sister, who is now a dancer, is one of the people most vulnerable to these policies. Her care is complicated and requires a strong medical team. When Medicaid is defunded, when climate change is ignored, when people with disabilities continue to be blamed for national crises — it is my sister and people like her who are among the first forgotten. That point that so many people are suffering and are not being heard — that's what keeps me going in my advocacy. We need to keep making sure that we are standing up for everybody, not just those in power or who have a microphone. When we all defy gravity, that is when we will see this world become a sky full of possibilities — when our hopes will take flight and we become the birds we were always destined to be.

The Resonance:

Suzanna's story is a powerful reminder that the impetus for changemaking begins with personal experience that extends into relationships with others, and eventually, into a desire to relieve the challenges and suffering of the community. We see the first inklings of her inclination towards the environmentally oriented SDGs in her exploration of nature with her sister; we see how her dedication towards health and public policy emerged from intense physical and mental hardship that she and her sister endured; and we see how her focus on education grew from her way of using knowledge as a means of growth and transcendence.

Through Suzanna's courageous vulnerability, we are able to see where the source of the SDGs come from – the gut-wrenching emotions evoked by suffering in personal and local lives. Suzanna illustrates the concept of moored in her choice to use the challenges she faced as fuel to become a beacon of positive change; and in remaining a changemaker, despite all the set-backs she actively encounters.

Her change-making journey began with local efforts: planting a communal garden, wreath laying at the cemetery, and tutoring other students. As she progressed throughout life and extended her reach, her policy efforts began to hone in on environmental oriented SDGs, such as SDG 13 (Climate Action), SDG 14 (Life Below Water), and particularly on SDG 15 (Life on Land). This is seen through her volunteer work in the Conservation Corps at Yellowstone, and then later as a farmhand in Australia. Her work on these SDGs was furthered through her involvement in *EnAct*, and expanded to encompass issues in SDGs 2 (Zero Hunger) and 11 (Sustainable Cities and Communities).

Although she continued in her efforts of conservation and sustainability, her focus began to shift towards public health, and in doing so, her work spread into the domain of SDG 3 (Good Health and Well-Being). Her discussion of the idea of *One Health* distinguishes itself as a 'systems-based approach' – which underscores the core essence of not only Suzanna's narrative, but also all the other narratives shared in this book. Efforts and progress in one domain of the SDGs are intertwined with the efforts and progress in other SDGs; these areas of life are dynamically interlinked with each other.

Though there are many achievements to remark on, it is crucial to demonstrate that through her unification of conservation and public health, her extension of advocacy across the globe and on different stages of policy is an excellent demonstration of SDG 17 (Partnership for the Goals). Suzanna's story is gripping, gut-wrenching, and inspiring.

As I sat on my bed and read Suzanna's words, the gravity of her sister's struggle felt like a physical weight on my chest and that same gut-wrenching feeling I felt on the street in my own city returned. It was not just a reaction to her sister's pain; it was a visceral response to the break in the web. When Suzanna speaks about the lack of access to healthcare, I feel she is not talking about a policy debate, she is talking about the "gravity" that keeps brilliant, stubborn people pinned to the ground. I realized then that my fight for Quality Education (SDG 4) and her fight for Good Health and Well-being (SDG 3) was the same battle: a refusal to let threads of our humanity be cut by neglect.

<u>**CHAPTER 5**</u>

The Pivot: "We Have Another Shot at Making the Right Decision"

Pivoting is not a change of strategy but a change of one's conscience. It requires a level of honesty that most systems are not built to handle. It means looking at your title, your project, your accolades and asking the relevant question: *Is this a bridge from a local reality to the capacity for change, or is it just a decoration?*

In July 2024, during a convening at the United Nations, I opened my remarks with a sentence I had not rehearsed: "Today we are at a gateway and we have another shot at making the right decision..." but I was only able to speak those un-rehearsed words because I was still moored from the experience on the school grounds, where I noticed the data-reality gap between reports and agricultural education in Sierra Leone. My remarks were not meant to be profound, nor were they born in the United Nations; they were born in the moment I was at those school grounds and realized that the 90% data was a ghost.

I was not just speaking to the people in the room; I was speaking for the strands that had been waiting for a decision since I first saw them snap. With that insight, I realized that choices delayed are still choices made. After the High-Level Political Forum, the moderator Corinna Hawkes, a Director at the Food and Agriculture Organization of the United Nations, later reflected publicly (on LinkedIn) that the phrase stayed with her as her favorite phrase of the event. Not because it was eloquent, but because it named something many of us were feeling: that history does not end when we get it wrong, but responsibility does not disappear either.

We don't pivot because we are restless. We pivot because staying still would be irresponsible. Oftentimes, some of us pretend biding our time is a neutral act, but in order to effectively pivot we have to stop waiting for the perfect conditions, and start working with the fractured threads we actually have. We have to stop asking for a seat at the table and start designing the room. It is the realization that "having another shot" means we must stop doing what has not worked and start reinforcing the strands that actually hold the weight.

The gateway may look different for every changemaker depending on where you stand in the spider web. For our global leaders in high-level rooms, the gateway to pivoting is a *point of policy*. It is where they decide to move beyond the 90% report and make choices that preserve our interest, protect the vulnerable, and represent the underrepresented. For them it is an institutional courage, moral, and integrity.

For you and me — the youth ambassadors, the delegates, the firebrands on the ground, whether you are a teacher, a student, a farmer, or a volunteer — the gateway to pivoting is a *point of survival*. It is where the spectacle of our titles ends and the reality of our service begins. It is the moment we stop performing for the microphone or camera and start being pragmatic about the causes we truly care about in our communities. It is the point where you volunteer not for the CV, but for the soil, for our planet. It is where we decide that even if the global thread remains broken, our local strands will not snap.

Of course, there are nuances in our roles, but whether we are moderating an event at the United Nations, holding a gavel in

New York, or a shovel in a school garden, we are standing at the same gateway. The director and the delegate are looking at the same fracture in the system. Our survival and our hope for a sustainable world are connected. If the leader fails to make the right decisions at the point of policy it affects our local representatives. The youth leader's point of survival becomes impossible. And if the youth and community leader stops weaving the soil, the global leader's policy becomes a ghost.

The gateway is where we are forced to look at each other. It is the only place where true change can happen, because spectacle cannot hide the reality to attain the sustainable world we have all been hoping for. We cannot pivot if we are still addicted to the spectacle. We have to be honest about whether we want the microphone or the impact. Pivoting requires a brutal audit of our own ego. We have to ask ourselves: *Am I here to be seen, or am I here to see the SDGs through? Am I just here to read reports and attend conferences; or am I here to represent, serve, and advocate for those who cannot?*

If you are there to see the SDGS through, you will pivot to the community the moment the stage becomes a distraction. You will pivot when pain and suffering unfold in our world and the rooms stay silent. You will pivot in the hours between conferences, turning talking points into tangible action while the rest of the world waits for the next agenda. You will pivot because you realize that this is an all-hands-on-deck job, and there is no room for gatekeeping when the structure — the sustainable world we are building together — is the only thing keeping us all from the fall.

And remember, when you are unsure of what to do, or where to begin, follow the gut-wrenching feeling. It is often the first and the last signal pointing you back to the truth.

CHAPTER 6

The Language we Carry

Oftentimes, the words we use shape what we see. The Sustainable Development Goals have names, but as mentioned in the previous chapters, we carry them as experiences and even our struggles. A slow response or lack of action is not a lack of passion, but rather a lack of language as tools for progress.

Below, is a spider web diagram with phrases that describe realities many of us recognize before we can name them; followed by a language exercise. This exercise is not about having the right answer, but about increasing awareness in your local realities where you are already connected.

Mapping the Strands

A language exercise, not a puzzle

When systems fail quietly, and people adapt instead of complain. This is often called: **NORMALIZED**

One who ignores hierarchy to connect broken strands between policy and people is a: **WEAVER**

The spaces between global commitments and lived consequences. We experience this as: **THE GAP**

The internal compass that signals when reality drifts too far from truth is known as: **GUT-WRENCH**

Progress in one SDG that weakens another. This is a **TRADE-OFF**

When participation becomes performed rather than practiced. It turns into: **SPECTACLE**

An honest assessment of our actions is called: **THE AUDIT**

An unwavering presence that ensures a global promise reaches local hands is: **ACCOUNTABILITY**

1. **Which of these words feel most familiar where you live?**

☐ Normalized

☐ The Gap

☐ Trade-off

☐ Gut-Wrench

☐ The Audit

☐ Spectacle

☐ Weaver

☐ Accountability

2. If this word or concept were a reality in your community, who do you think would feel it first and who would feel it last?

3. **Which Sustainable Development Goal does this word most closely relate to in your context and which other goals does it quietly impede?**

4. **What actions within your immediate control could this concept be reinforced to support the SDGS, without waiting for permission or a platform?**

____

____

____

____

____

____

____

____

____

____

____

____

____

____

5. What structures can be put in place or actions can we
    take to ensure people remain accountable for their
    commitment to sustainability?

6. When you stand at the gateway of pivoting, who do you see standing with you? Which individuals can you collaborate with to promote progress and foster Sustainable Development Goals?

Works Cited

Oprah Winfrey. *The Path Made Clear : Discovering Your Life's Direction and Purpose*. New York, Flatiron Books, 2019, pp. 44, 45.

Obama, Michelle, and Craig Robinson. *Disappointment Is the Key to Career Success with Keke Palmer*. Higher Ground Productions, 26 Mar. 2025, podcasts.apple.com/us/podcast/disappointment-is-the-key-to-career-success-with/id1532956108?i=1000700896244. Podcast.

AUTHOR

Joseph Bangura is a former educator, television presenter, and currently a youth ambassador with the United Nations Major Group for Children and Youth whose work bridges local realities to global development conversation through. He has contributed to international policy conversations through his engagement with the United Nations Major Group for Children and Youth and has participated in global forums like the United Nations ECOSOC Partnership Forum, and Food and Agricultural Organization of the United Nations High Level Political Forum as a youth speaker and rapporteur. Through community-led projects such as school-based education initiatives and youth leadership programs, Joseph focuses on connecting local realities with global development conversations highlighting the power of everyday leadership and role of young people in shaping more just and sustainable societies.

CO-AUTHOR/EDITOR

Noah Dennie is a teacher at a small charter school in South Tucson with a bachelor degree in Philosophy. His background in Philosophy has brought a unique depth to this project. He didn't just edit words; he challenged my thinking, helped me expand my vision, and ensured this book would truly resonate with the next generation of leaders. After receiving supportive aid from his community earlier in life, he has committed himself to strengthening different foundations of communal support. For now, that is aimed towards struggling youth; eventually he hopes to become a psychologist. He spends his time studying, exercising, and walking his dog, Harley.